in the
college
at night

ALSO BY BRYANT A. LONEY

Exodus in Confluence

—

A NOVELLA

To Hear the Ocean Sigh

—

A NOVEL

Take Me to the Cat

—

A NOVEL

Sea Breeze Academy

—

A NOVEL

in the *college* at night

Poems by
BRYANT A. LONEY

Published by PEPPERNELL
Copyright © 2019 by Bryant A. Loney

All rights reserved. No part of this book may be used or performed without written consent from the author, except for critical articles or reviews. Please do not participate in or promote electronic piracy of copyrighted materials.
Please support the author's rights and purchase only authorized editions.

Peppernell is in residence in Fayette, Alabama, by the backing of Luxapalila Creek, a gathering place designed to help writers and artists create and produce. Peppernell books are published and distributed by Verona Booksellers.

Our titles may be purchased in bulk at special quantity discounts for promotional, educational, or business use. Book excerpts can also be created
to fit specific needs. For details, write: info@veronabooksellers.com.

ISBN 978-0-9971700-4-7 (trade paperback)
ISBN 978-0-9971700-5-4 (e-book)

"The Girl with the Answers" and "Thinking Ahead and Back Again" first appeared in The University of Tulsa's *Stylus* Student Journal of Art and Writing, volume 17, 2018.

Tattoo illustration by Allyson Kotarsky (Ballyvaughan, County Clare, Ireland)
www.instagram.com/ally.kotarsky

"Letting Go" and "Graduation Afternoon" borrow and adapt lines from Alex Dimitrov's *Together and by Ourselves*.

Cover and book design by Inkstain Design Studio
First Edition: April 2019

10 9 8 7 6 5 4

*For years, we joked about this dedication,
what I would write, would say,
admit. But I can't keep this promise
to you, just like so many before.*

And as the smart ship grew
In stature, grace, and hue,
In shadowy silent distance
    grew the iceberg too.

    —THOMAS HARDY,
    "The Convergence of the Twain."

I hope the exit is joyful
and I hope to never return.

    —FRIDA KAHLO,
    final words in her diary.

TABLE OF CONTENTS

I. OLD HEART

To the Reader	1
Everything I Never Said	2
Proximity	4
October	5
Darker	6
At the End of Everything	7
Text Junkie	8
Voicemails	9
Lightning Bugs on the Porch	12
Longest Night	13
Cold Comfort	14
Against the Rocks	15
Nighttime House Call	16
Changing of the Seasons	17
Unknowable	18
Band Practice	19
Lines on the Loss of a Relationship	20
Make It Last	21
Sleeping	22

II. SEARCHING

Waking Up	25
The Hole at the Center of Everything	26
Memories, Part One	27

The Girl with the Answers	29
Shorter Days, Longer Nights	32
The Light We Cast	33
Cycles	34
To Making a New Friend by Mentioning Free Pizza…	35
On Seeing the Girl You Like…	36
Art History	38
Like Ships	39
Restless	40
Fall Fair	41
Grapefruit Sky	42
Everything Feels Bigger and Smaller	43
A First Date	44
Creeping Distress	45
Cent'anni	46
Thinking Ahead and Back Again	47
Lost and Found	48
Feathers	49
This Sacred Line	50
Pulsating Ambience	51
Night Owl	52
Living with High-Functioning Depression	53
Sorry Sorry Sorry	54
We Write the Words; We Live Them	58
Tasteless	59
Really Drunk	60
I'm Going to Break Something	62
Another Warm Body	63
Having Fun	64
Shopping at Age Seventeen vs. Twenty-One	66
Searching the Past	67

Echoes	68
Since We Saw Each Other Last	69
A Glimpse of the Other World	70
Monologue	71
Roommates	72
White Tee	74
We Are Artists; Always Changing	76
Land of Green and Gold	77
Memories, Part Two	80
Roach	83
The Wind Can Be Still	84
Riverboat Toads	85
Fell for the Wrong Girl	87
Letting Go	88

III. NEW HEART

Best Available Friends	93
Tropicala	94
The Silliest and Softest of Dreams	95
Weighted Warmth	96
Type	97
Different Persons	98
Dulcinea	99
Shadows Take Me Back	100
This Fear of Mine	101
Two Displays	102
Together	103
Love is Not an Instagram Poem	105
Christmas Eve Eve	107
White Tee (Reprise)	110

Longer Days, Shorter Nights	112
Scene: A Mediterranean Restaurant by the River…	113
Graduation Afternoon	114
AZ	117
Serenity	118
The Exit is Joyful	119
Epilogue	120

in the
college
at night

I. OLD HEART

TO THE READER

I am confident, or not, I am.
I speak to you, I speak to you,
and I am not talking to you.
No colors and semicolons here.
No room for underlining
simple things: <u>love</u> and <u>love</u>.
No, I speak at night.
No results. No love.
Good living? It's fine.
Yes, I am gone,
and there is a fire;
watch me burn.

EVERYTHING I NEVER SAID

To my dazzling datemate on her 18th birthday:

    It knocks me out how long I've known you
    and how long we've been together.
    When we met, you danced for me.
    I showed you embarrassing pictures of myself,
    and I got you to stop crying.
    The years have unfolded beautifully,
    and throughout all our adventures,
    I have grown more in love with you
    than I ever thought possible.
    You make me excited.

    I love your hands
    and how they always drift instinctively to mine.
    I love your eyes
    and how they fit into the gaze of my own.
    I love how you think of every corgi as ours,
    and that you look out for me,
    and that you hold me when I want you to.
    You are my flower, my absolute rose,
    and you have given my life more beauty
    than I could have ever asked for.
    You've made me feel wondrous
    and made yourself a permanent bed in my brain.

I never want you to leave.

Thank you for being with me when I'm sad.
Thank you for being so perfect and magnificent for me.
I know that we both try so hard for each other,
and it makes me so grateful.
We're not running away from things;
we're inviting things in. This amazing thing we have—
it makes me feel less afraid the longer we're together.
I'm crazy for you. I adore you.
To two years, and all the rest.

"Happy birthday."

PROXIMITY

The sheets are pushed.
Your mom is listening.
Bottles of wine and pizza boxes.
Your legs around my waist.

I'm not ready for a real life.
That much I know.
Only dreams and future schemes.
A scream inside a scream.

OCTOBER

What an awful way to die:
without hesitating or   looking

                    at the cost,
drinking something from a shot glass,
reminding me of the day
when I followed you   out

                    of the kitchen,
and we sat in near silence,
an autumn chill to our bodies,   for you,

                  for me,
a feeling I never quite understood,   a feeling I never quite understood.

DARKER

You argued with your mother
this one time—
something trivial, with laughter.
With a half-smile,
she turned to me
and said,

"Don't you ever wish you could just choke her?"

There were nights I did.
There were nights you let me.
Hard.

AT THE END OF EVERYTHING

What jealous moon calms this tide for but a moment
to reunite sea and shore with longing and joy
                          and it's so good
                                  to see you
                          and I missed you
                                  so much
                          and I'm sorry for
                          and I love you
                          and I love you too
                          and
                  no—
         wait—
   please—

Come back.

TEXT JUNKIE

Hey, wanna hang?
8/21 7:16 p.m.

When is the party?
8/27 3:28 p.m.

Hey, what's up?
9/01 1:10 a.m.

Happy birthday…
9/28 9:34 a.m.

heyy whats
3/22 1:55 a.m.

Congratulations.
5/21 7:16 p.m.

(…)

VOICEMAILS

You're just driving home right now,
you say, and you were just, like,
thinking about me. You don't know why.
Not, like, in a bad way, you mean—
like, you just started thinking about me,
for some reason.
Just… wanted to call me
before you forget to.
'Cause you've been meaning to lately,
but things have been so crazy
with the end of school and everything,
like… it's just been so nuts,
you say. So you thought you would
call me and let me know that
you're thinking about me
and you hope I'm doing really well
and we should totally get coffee soon
and catch up because it's been forever,
so, just… have a nice night.

Hey, you tell me. You're so sorry
we keep missing each other.
You were napping earlier,
and you totally lost track of time
and slept for, like, four hours,

so you missed my call,
and you're really sorry…
But you'd still love to talk,
if I'm still available. So…
Talk soon. Bye.

Hey, you whisper. You—
you know I'm at work and, umm,
you know that—you know—
that this might not be the best time,
but, just, if I wanted to hear something
after… umm.
You're sorry you didn't get back to me
earlier. You were just…
You just didn't really know what to say.
You don't really know, like,
how to do this? You're as lost as I am.
You… don't really know what the proper
etiquette is… right now.
You just don't know… how to handle this.
So… you whisper that I'm not a mess.
That I am… a very strong, capable
human being. I am… a good person.
And… I'm… going to be okay.
And… we're going to be okay,
as, like, friends. And you know
it seems like you're ignoring me,
and you're not meaning to be.
You just… don't know how to handle this,
umm, in the right way.
And you hope I understand that

if you don't answer, it's just because
you don't know what to say or, like,
how to say it well, umm,
and it's really got nothing to do with me.
It's just that you don't know…
how to say…
don't know what you want to say.
You're sorry, you whisper.
You, umm… you're thinking about me.
If I need to talk—

LIGHTNING BUGS ON THE PORCH

I drove by your home and saw the boxes.
There was a big van and a sign reading:
SOLD. I frowned, thought, to whom?

I hope the new kids find that spot
where you almost burned the house down
and the stains from all the wine
we spilled and tried to cover up.
May they say, "This is where her parents
repainted her room while she was with her
grandma in Colorado. Over here is where
her dog threw up at his feet the first
time he came over. Oh, was she mortified.
There, she trembled during thunderstorms.
And there, they talked about the future."
What they won't see is our smiles. Not
because that's between us, but because
those photos faded long before.

Echoes only go so far.
So far, it's not so good.

LONGEST NIGHT

Sorry
for
the
times
I
didn't
hold
you
longer.

COLD COMFORT

There's a box of stuff for you
in the attic. Things I kept
in case we ever…

A mug with hearts on the side.
A mixtape with all our songs.
A t-shirt from that one vacation.
I could go on.

Label the box, "Keepsakes."
Bury me inside.
Float us out to   sea.

AGAINST THE ROCKS

Does the sea at night look familiar?
Does it take you back?

The stars, out and quivering,
almost terrifyingly dark
in the black nothingness.
But also the widest smile
we ever shared,
                drifting
on our own reflection.

To hear the ocean sigh.
To sleep in spite of sea.

NIGHTTIME HOUSE CALL

Not even in my dreams do you stay.
It's not like I ask for this.
I don't sit in bed to bargain and beg,
"Please, Lord, give me another chance…"
To watch her laugh, to hear her smile,
to feel your words against my hands
until I am pulled from you into this
thunderstorm outside, the whirling winds,
the sound of some lone hawk or alarm,
always stretching me further away
from your heart, I wish to feel,
one more time, please.

You, you said people don't change.
I did.

CHANGING OF THE SEASONS

I talked in my sleep last night
to thank you in a dream.
You looked so peaceful.
Forgive me for waking.

It's raining.
It's been raining.
I don't know why
I'm writing you.
It's not all about
me,
I swear.

You left gray in my hair.
Doesn't matter anymore.
Kind of like the look, even.
Distinguished. Older.
Wiser.

People stopped asking about you.
Maybe I should too.

UNKNOWABLE

If I squint my eyes like this, I see
two of us, you and me, in that mirror.
One couple will go the route we took.
They'll laugh for a long while,
then they'll stop for even longer.
They will sort of try again,
but then they'll move on, away.

This other pair, though—
they will do great things together.
They will travel, they will explore,
they will not stop when satisfied.
They will paint pretty words and
they will write songs in every color.
They will be the good example.

Here's to them, who we never met.
Here's to them, who we left behind.

B AND PRACTICE

Let's start up a band, you said.
Call it "Goth, Paper, Scissors."
That was maybe four years ago,
and holy cow, has it been that long?
Anyway, the band. You could play
the saxophone, me on vocals.
Not much for a punk group.
Still, you were pretty adamant,
or more like pretty-comma-adamant,
as in both stunning and stubborn—
so yeah, Goth, Paper, Scissors
recorded their first and only single
in your bathroom in late 2013.
The people reading this poem,
they'll never hear our music.
They should be grateful. Awful stuff.
But I remember you getting into it,
the way you swayed your hair
to the song in your head,
and I'm so glad I was there
for that show of ours.

LINES ON THE LOSS OF A RELATIONSHIP

Darling,

I hate myself, but more important, I miss you.
This isn't a love confession—but it is.
I wish I hadn't gotten so mean to protect myself.
I wish you could hear what I whisper in the dark:
everything I'd always wanted to say,
lines so well-rehearsed. Something tragic.
I lose the words so easily. Ideas fade away.
Should've sent those late-night texts.

We were best friends. You were always there,
and yet I never understood why.
I'm a coward, glacial and stark.
I lie on the kitchen floor,
awake but too tired to think.
And past these empty rooms and weak ceilings,
I see you, in the strange orange of my memories.
Ashes to ashes; stardust to stardust.

I know exactly what to say. Only took a year.
I never lost this love for you.
I would really like to go back to the beach with you.

MAKE IT LAST

Hold her in your arms,

look out the bedroom window,

and smile at the music that's playing.

Indie folk, in all likelihood.

Learn all the ways to make her laugh,

how her eyes make you feel like

an endless summer together.

Cherish these moments.

Talk about nothing in particular.

SLEEPING

"You didn't say
good night."

"It wasn't."

———————

Last, I get into my bed,
scream as loud as possible,
and then I fall asleep.

II. SEARCHING

WAKING UP

I woke up early in the morning
to shout at night's death.

I dreamed of having dreamed my dreams,
hoping that I would find a day
to ask
what I
could see.

THE HOLE AT THE CENTER OF EVERYTHING

~~I don't expect you to know something if I don't post about it, and I don't expect you to ask how I'm doing, feeling, what my worries are at nineteen.~~ But know this:
I do believe in God,
the breakup did get easier,
I never got the dog I wanted,
and this new novel almost killed me.
Now? ~~Breathe. Forgive. Laugh. Here.~~
Onward.

MEMORIES, PART ONE
(After Joe Brainard's *I Remember*)

What I remember?

I remember wanting to be a Caribbean pirate when I grew up.

I remember having to wait for the VHS to rewind all the way before I could watch the tape again.

I remember a girl having a crush on me in preschool and naming her goldfish after me.

I remember seeing movies twice in theaters—once with family, again with friends.

I remember watching TV shows starring action figures and then wanting my mom to buy me those toys for Christmas.

But I also remember not being able to play outside for a couple of years because we lived in bad apartments.

I remember being the last of my classmates to finish our timed multiplication worksheets.

I remember teasing a kid in fifth grade for reading *Harry Potter*.

And I remember getting mad at Mario's capabilities when I was actually mad with my own.

That's what I remember.

THE GIRL WITH THE ANSWERS
(Adapted from *Take Me to the Cat*)

I want to talk to Catherine, but Bryce threw this party to film his music video, so he has me with Gabby by the pool. I don't not like Gabby, she's okay, but I really like Catherine, and I think she likes me back. She's sitting with Christian and Belle. I'm with Gabby. Gabby talks about her trip to California. I can't hear what Catherine is saying.

There are a couple of cameras around, though we're not supposed to look at them. No one's controlling the cameras because it's meant to all be natural. Bryce is good with video, good with singing, good looking too. Better than me. I think Gabby is here for Bryce, or maybe Christian or the other guy, who are also in Bryce's band. They're called Gender. They're great.

Gabby says she met a famous actor while she was hiking in California. She says his name twice, but I miss it both times. She tries again, but I swear I don't know him. She says he was in that one movie. I still don't know him. She frowns. Bryce from across the pool tells Gabby not to frown. She laughs instead.

Catherine wades through the water to get to me. I like her eyes best. She takes my hands and pulls me in. It's cold, but she's inviting, so I shake it off. She gestures with her head to Bryce, who sits in a lounge chair and mouths the lyrics to his song for one of the cameras. She turns back to me and then goes under. I follow.

I open my eyes and see her reaching between my legs. I feel her grip, and I tense up. She smiles, and tiny bubbles escape from her nose. She resurfaces, and so do I.

Bryce is saying he thinks he got enough footage and everyone can go take a fifteen-minute break. Catherine pulls herself out of the pool, readjusts her swimsuit, and then joins the others inside. I wait awhile in the water. It's chilly for August, but that's okay. We leave for college in a month.

I get out, and Bryce pulls me aside. He says he's got some people, some business people, who think he can get twenty thousand views on this music video in the first week.
He wants to use this to convince Christian and the other guy to stay in town to work on Gender. I say I wish them luck.
He says he doesn't need luck but views. I suggest a crappy filter over the video to make it look like it's being played from a VHS tape. He says he likes the way I think.

Inside, Catherine is chatting with Gabby and Belle.
The girls laugh, and then Catherine notices me.
She smiles first with her eyes and then her lips.
She walks down the hall, and I follow.

We're in the bathroom. She kisses me hard, and it's less sexy than it is painful against my teeth, but I pull her closer anyway, and we push against the counter. She coughs on my neck, and I grab her lower back. Someone outside tries the door handle, but it's locked, so we continue.

A minute later, I'm holding on to the shower rod while Catherine is on her knees. I'm trying to remember that famous guy's name, the one from the movie, but I can't. I don't know if I should know him or if he's only been in indie films, and so then it's okay if I haven't seen him, but not really. Bryce would know, probably, or those business people. It's not even that good of a song.

Catherine uses some toilet paper to clean up, and then we leave the bathroom. Bryce, Christian, and the other guy are looking over one of the cameras. Bryce says it was pointed the wrong way, and so we'll have to go back out and do it again. Christian scratches his head, then says that's fine, and he goes outside with Catherine and Belle.

Gabby joins me by the pool. I ask her the name of that famous guy from the movie, but she wants to tell me about this poetry she's been reading instead. Bryce says something about losing daylight. I can't hear what Catherine is saying.

SHORTER DAYS, LONGER NIGHTS

I long for autumn,
that sweet fall:
crisp air, cider,
companionship,
something to do.

~~I wish I was better at making friends.~~
I wish I was better at keeping friends.

Summer,
lying
on the
ground,
bright
red
with
anxiety.

THE LIGHT WE CAST

There are people I kind of knew
(—but also sort of didn't—)
who I think about from time to time.
They won't be reading this. Still,
I often wonder how they're doing,
how their relationship is going,
where they went to college,
what they study, what they do for fun,
what they thought of me in high school.
We might've been friends, had the stars
aligned. Different circles, I guess.
But in that universe, I'm glad we met.
Let's stay close, all right?

CYCLES

I know how to make myself silent,
how to make it so my bones don't creak
and the floorboards don't wake.
Since I was eight, I've done this.
I have listened, I have spied,
I have learned more than any son
should know about his domestic space.
There were tears. Not mine.
Revelations. Not mine.
This is not a perfect home.
I should take comfort in knowing
there are none, but that doesn't help.
And tomorrow? Is just another Tuesday.
So send forth your chariots of likes,
your baskets of well wishes.
(Thank you. I do appreciate them all.)
But maybe this year, instead of the
enthusiastic "Happy Birthday,"
say: "You did good. You did."
Because I am tired. And I tried.
So hard, for so long.

TO MAKING A NEW FRIEND
BY MENTIONING FREE PIZZA,
AND THE GIRL WALKING BY IS LIKE,
DID YOU SAY FREE PIZZA?

Getting back into the groove of things,
this whole college business. Bleh.
Always rushing to places, the breathing,
and eating on the go.
But I do want to say,
in this spare moment we're sharing,
Hey. It's nice to see you again.
I thought of you over the summer,
and I wanted to reach out,
but when I call people on the phone,
they think I'm weird or mistaken
or in love with them… you know.
So. Here's to the new semester.
See you around, yeah?

ON SEEING THE GIRL YOU LIKE WALKING THROUGH THE COLLEGE CAMPUS

You see her walking across campus
with that walk of hers, that kind of walk,
you know the one.
You noticed it the first time,
and it stands out again to you now.
Is it something with the shoulders?
Oh shit, she saw you—
just then—staring at her—
or did she? The sun—in your eyes—
you were squinting
the sun out of your eyes, you would say.
Doesn't matter, shouldn't matter.
You don't want to give the wrong idea,
that she might think you're into her
in more than just that
we-had-that-one-class-together-freshman-year
sort of way.
She's not your type, remember?
She's too this and too that.
Reminds you of so-and-so from high school,
or that actor you saw on TV
when you were home for the break,

when Mom kept asking about grades
and your major and whether you are seeing—

And there she goes with that walk of hers,
and it doesn't matter what you were thinking
because she'll never know,
I'll never know,
and nobody will ever know,
and she'll forever stay on your
Recommended Friends list
because you keep letting her walk on by,
walk on by,
walk on walking on.

ART HISTORY

Art history class at the university,
no one's paying attention.
Some naked women on the screen—
can't react, that's not professional.
Girl two rows down and to the left
is shopping for shoes online.
Guy next to her scrolls through
a slideshow for some other class.
Guy in front of me wears a t-shirt
promoting his fraternity.

Prof asks a question along the lines of,
"Has anyone here ever seen…?"
Fill in the blank, doesn't matter;
we all shake our heads no,
even if we have;
we don't want Prof to speak to us.

Defeated, he moves on.
Girl buys another pair.

LIKE SHIPS

Three months after you left,
it used to be, in my mind,
"I miss you so much."
Then a year and a half arrived,
and it became simply, merely,
"I miss you."
Today I see you in the third row,
dressed up, smiling wide,
a tear for our bride and groom.
We make eyes. We talk.
It's as if no time has passed.
Now I sit here, writing this.
And I miss you so much.

RESTLESS

I had this dream where
I went up to you in public
and you saw me,
and we smiled,
and you had clear skin,
and you were happy I noticed.
We talked about college,
books you're reading for fun—
and then I woke up.
Hope all is well.

FALL FAIR

Where in the carnival
would you place me? Beside the
strong man for laughs,
or the clown for comparison?
The bearded lady,
to shame me?
The apple bobbing trough,
to drown me?
No, please: let me read palms
and tell fortunes.
I'm good at making stuff up.

GRAPEFRUIT SKY

They call her "Gypsy van Grrl."
Part-time mermaid, '80s fashion.
She's in with the in crowd,
says, "Be kind to yourself
and the world." She's a hero —
a black hole, sucking you in,
and you never want to leave her.
Killer at Spotify playlists.
Un viaje a alguna parte.
But she's not going your way.
Nah, she's a summer babe,
and you're a bummer, babe.
West coastin'. Wild child.

EVERYTHING FEELS BIGGER AND SMALLER

We were sorry once,
apologizing for everything,
regretting what we'd said.
We were sorry.
We believed in each other.
We thought things would be different.
We were sorry.
We were seventeen.

I want to go
somewhere warm,
but then
I'll want to be
somewhere cold.
It's a dilemma,
you see.

New love
replaces old:
these feelings
transferred
yet remain
in a permanent,
haunting silence.

A FIRST DATE

We look at each other a certain way.
(I'm not sure how I feel,
I'm thinking of ending things—)
She asks questions. I answer.
I ask questions. She answers.
Funny how it works like that.
Comforting too.
(Too comforting?)
Smile. (Smile.)

CREEPING DISTRESS

Last night, I got this sense of dread
wondering if things were all right
between us. You said we're good,
there's nothing to worry about,
and that all is well with the world.
Yet your eyes now stare out different
windows, and you stir your coffee
clockwise instead of counter.
Counter. Count her? Count on her.
Nothing to fear. All in my head.
Thank God you can't see the real me.

                        All I need?
For you to kiss my forehead and whisper
all the good things left in the universe.

CENT'ANNI

You were leaving for Italy, you said.
Five months. Then we'll see.
If it's meant to be, it will.
Well, dammit, it wasn't.
And here we are, way past then.
Yet in the pictures, you look happy.
Who am I to disagree?

THINKING AHEAD AND BACK AGAIN

Choosing the wasteland over the coast:
a new fear at age twenty.
Never meeting who you were
supposed to in college,
or ignoring the ones you did.

When we're no longer speaking,
send me a song.
I'll listen this time, I swear it.
To the weekend heart.
To the weakened heart.

LOST AND FOUND

A silver necklace with a black heart
pendant, sapphire in the right light,
found near the Fisher West suites.
Who gave it to you? The black heart.
Your boyfriend, before the breakup?
Your best friend, before they found
her sprawled out in the tub?
Or did you buy it for yourself
after your mother called, crying
as she whispered, "I have cancer."
Did it fall from your neck by mistake
while chaining your bike to the post?
Or did you leave it here on purpose,
so tired of its memories and bruises.

(He laughs.) Who are we kidding?
This isn't about the necklace anymore.
And yet I wonder… was it ever?

FEATHERS

A strand of your hair on my old sweater.
I know it's yours because it's pink.
You would get so cold at night, and
the sweater looked better on you anyway.
You didn't keep it after our breakup;
you kept the fake bugs I bought for you
to hide around your apartment,
your bedroom, under my pillow,
because I know your sense of humor.
Wish somebody would figure out mine.
So while it's true I'm still unsure
why some bugs bite and not others,
you are every pink-haired girl I see—
these chills of mine less random than
I thought.

THIS SACRED LINE

When I saw you in my home that night,
I was scared (of what you might say,
do, think of me and these verses on the
walls that preach about a familial love
we are assumed to have from birth).
You sat away from the rest of them,
taking it all, taking me, in.
As I introduced to you the kitchen,
living room, den, and bedroom,
did you see Christmases, birthdays,
ex-girlfriends, summer nights,
and a novel's worth of forgive me please?
Or did you understand that for a moment,
I could outdistance those memories
and imagine an alternate timeline
of this only.

If vulnerability is unattractive,
then I'm the ugliest one of all.

Thank you,
& good night.

PULSATING AMBIENCE

Your arm around a person
is a special place to be.
I'm not talking about
some pose for selfies.
I mean with tears, silence,
and shaky breaths and night.
Intimate. The calm.
It's her trusting you with
her parents' divorce,
her fear of sex,
her worries about moving
back to college on the coast
and what it means to be in a
long-distance relationship.
Intimate. The calm.
Don't mess that up.

NIGHT OWL

Sometimes I pretend it's mid-July.
That I can still call you,
randomly at night, to talk
for four hours about God and life:

> Your mother tells you to keep it down,
> so you whisper for a minute.
> But then you bubble with excitement—
> about Broadway, dark chocolate,
> Thomas Hardy, Julie Andrews—
> and gosh, it's full volume again,
> and I'm smiling on my end,
> and we're laughing away our anxieties,
> no matter sleep schedules and work
> and rehearsal in the morning.
> Intimate. The calm.

But it's November.
I'm at our special place, alone.
And though your friends gave me advice,
no one asked if I was ready.

LIVING WITH HIGH-FUNCTIONING DEPRESSION

I am not sad. At least, you'll never
see me like that. I decided long ago
someone has to be the morning person,
full of pep, personality, persona.
It's exhausting. It's not healthy.
It's how I make friends.
I am better now,
but you would never know.
You'll never hear me
talk about suffering.
Weekends are always good.
Work is always good.
School is always good.
Me? I change the subject.
I am not sad. But I am not happy.

SORRY SORRY SORRY

I'm at this party because I was invited. Esther's in my class on protest literature, and she liked what I had to say on James Baldwin. So she invited me to her Christmas party. I think this is funny because I know she is Jewish.

I know she is Jewish because I looked her up beforehand. Of course. The guy I thought was her boyfriend is in fact her gay roommate Drew. Drew is very gay. Esther is single. Esther is nice. But there's something off about her—something with her never wearing any makeup. Some girls don't, especially at an eight a.m. But never? She's short, like me. I'm taller by an inch. But she's always coughing, and why doesn't she cover her mouth? Just coughs to the side, like I can't see her, like I'm not always watching.

The wreath on the apartment door is blue and silver. My car is in the parking lot. I could leave. We're playing a variation of spin the bottle—Esther, Mason, Shani, and me, all classmates. The bottle lands on Mason. Esther draws a card. It says Mason must either share his most embarrassing sex story or take a drink. Mason looks down at his glass of box wine.

He says they were in her car, parked in the lot behind their high school. There was a security camera. Her father was the principal. Esther laughs. It's more of a snort. Drew joins the game and smiles at her. Shani is already drunk and giggling.

Mason spins the bottle. Drew. It says Mason must give Drew a lap dance while somebody films. Drew grins. Mason shakes his head no and then takes the drink for him. Esther does that laugh again. Drew rolls his eyes and spins, but it points to the door, where nobody's sitting. Drew spins again.

Would I give Drew a lap dance? If the card said to, that is. What even is a lap dance? What happens? Those videos, they aren't the kind I watch, and I've never been to one of those places where they happen.

I look up and Shani is talking about the time she tripped so hard on acid she thought her back was pulsating colors—neon pinks, greens, blues. Shani shrugs and spins. Esther: either text your ex or drink.

Drew frowns. Esther fidgets with her glass, almost empty, twice refilled. Drew is about to say something when Esther downs the last of the red wine. It spills down her cheek. She wipes it with the back of her hand and spins.

I watch. I try to move it with my mind, but it lands on me. Esther smiles. She draws a card.

She says for me to kiss her. Mason says I could also drink. She grins a lopsided grin, her teeth caked in crimson and maybe too big for her mouth. I grip my glass, turn it over.

Esther is obviously upset. She asks if I really won't kiss her. Mason looks at me, as does Drew. Shani is elsewhere. I blurt out something about that online course we took. The one about sexual assault. The mandatory one. I stammer.
I say she's drunk, she can't consent.

It's a kiss, she insists. She says for me to kiss her.
Drew tells me to just kiss her, man.

I remember a statistic, most likely from the Internet, about how the average person sleeps with eight partners in a lifetime. It's been well over a year since I've had sex. I've been on dates, but things have been quiet lately. Nothing much has happened, but something could, tonight, if I wanted.

Esther stands, saying it's fine, it's whatever. She hiccups. She repeats herself. She goes into the room that isn't Drew's or the bathroom, so it must be hers. She slams the door. I imagine following Esther inside, us taking off our clothes, her lying on her back—the one she's complained about in class on rainy days—me putting on a condom, me slipping inside her, her head back, her eyes closed, her suddenly coughing to the side.

Drew gets up to go check on her. Mason fidgets with his glass before setting it on the coffee table. Shani is asleep on the couch. I leave. I tell Mason goodbye, and Mason nods, and then I'm into December again. I cross my arms over my chest and then look around for my car.

No. No, I shouldn't have ignored her like that. I should have kissed her like a man. Esther is nice, warm, inviting, and I shouldn't have done that. I'm such an idiot. Why didn't I just kiss her? It wouldn't have killed me. I'm sorry, I will say. I'm so sorry, Esther. Sorry sorry sorry. Would you please forgive me, the idiot, please.

I go back to knock on the door when I notice the lights through the blinds into Esther's room. Esther lies sideways on the bed, crying into her sheets, her pants down, and Drew is standing with his jeans around his ankles, in and out of her, glancing up at the ceiling, as if this were habit for them.

Mason opens the front door with Shani stumbling behind him. He's taking her back to her dorm. Shani groans at the concrete. Mason pats her back. They leave, but for now, I stay behind. I watch through the blinds, the cold to my back, wondering what Baldwin would say in a moment like this.

WE WRITE THE WORDS; WE LIVE THEM

She tells me to kill my darlings.
It's her way of breaking up.
It's an old writing tip,
from one writer to another:
get rid of what you love most.
She falls for words more than I do,
and she's unafraid to tell me
there's too much exposition here,
not enough variance there.
She gets what I do, gets me.
And she understands,
the sentence began,
these novels don't write themselves.
There's always a muse: an *exodus*,
an *ocean*, a *cat*. Heartbreak.
Writing a novel is telling a joke
and no one laughs for two years.
Kill my darlings. Kill my darling.
Writing can be so lonely.

TASTELESS

Gaudy liquor,
champagne corks,
I don't know
if I can love like that
anymore.

———————————

Add me
to your
wine
and drink me
whole.

REALLY DRUNK (WHEN IT'S 99¢ MARGS AND YOU HAVE NO SELF-CONTROL)

It's so dumb that there are over
1,000 different beetle types in the world
who needs that many
who even cares
I guess entomologists need a job
but still
oh well
while we're inventing things
and creating civilizations
beetles are just adding new species
that are the same
but with different wing
patterns. They're trying their best
by not trying at all
Something to admire

Who else is tired of the whole
existing thing

me
I am

It's hard
& I want to go home

Please run me over
72 times
until I am *pulp*

        Do emos still exist
        or is it just that everybody wants to die now

I was that kid in kindergarten
with the full set of crayons
in 64 colors
It didn't make me feel better though
it always made me feel out of place
and so I begged my mom
to buy me the cheaper brand
with just 8 colors in a box
so I could fit in with everyone else
childhood is weird
I also lied about being a vampire
but that's unrelated

This class ends
in approximately two hours
I love you
Drink more water
Sit up straight

I'M GOING TO BREAK SOMETHING

I am a wild animal at the zoo
and you're peering right into the glass
and I see you on the other side
and I'm getting ready to charge at you
until I hit the glass
and you are going to scream so loud
at the impact.

I am absolutely out of my limits
and tearing my hair out.
You can't stop me.

I am all wound up
and ready to lose my mind.

ANOTHER WARM BODY

This is at a college campus party.
I'm twenty-one and so are you.
We take sips of our drinks
and banter back and forth.
My hand is in your hair,
your fingers on my chest.
We're lost,
lost in the middle of the crowd,
lost in the rapidity of life.
We're lost,
but it is right here where I am,
going slow when I look into your eyes,
going fast when I kiss you,
going to our own time,
both of us unafraid and not embarrassed
to try new things.
And it doesn't matter if I love you
or if you love me back—
if we wanted the truth,
we wouldn't be here.
So we move forward with what remains,
straddling adulthood and childhood.
We're lost. Without limits. Do anything,
to feel anything, at all.

HAVING FUN

Daniel thinks it would be fun to burn all the money we have on us. An anti-capitalist middle finger to the systemic oppression against us meager college students. Philosophy and power systems. Stumbling over words. So, way too drunk and with no hope of coming back, we hand over our ones and fives and twenties, we take Zoey's lighter, and we set the cash aflame.

Jenna returns then with Daniel's car keys. The bills are burning in a touristy pot from a Yucatán vacation. She screams at us from the front door, calling us a bunch of fucking idiots and mentioning several biblical figures by first name.

Daniel laughs at her. We laugh at her.

Jenna asks how we possibly thought this was a good idea. She asks how we're going to pay for Lyla's graduation gift or that summer road trip to San Valla. She talks about her tuition, her GPA, the three jobs she has to work to keep studying here— and we're just gonna burn our money like that? In an on-campus apartment? On a school night?

Daniel stops laughing. He tells her to leave if she's going to be this way. She says this is her apartment too, you know. Daniel says it's a majority rule. He looks at us expectantly, and we nod. So Jenna should either change into her swimsuit and float in the kiddie pool with Shani and Colin in the other room, or leave. It's really that simple. We nod that it really is that simple.

Jenna looks from Daniel to the baggies of coke on her coffee table, shakes her head, and then leaves. Daniel claps as she does so. He then turns to us, arms wide and raised. He asks who's ready for more shots. With our faces illuminated by the flames, we say, we are.

SHOPPING AT AGE SEVENTEEN VS. TWENTY-ONE

Then, our hushed laughter. Hurried whispers.
Searching the Internet for "girth length"
and thinking about it. Different flavors.
Ribbed for pleasure? Also, some candy
and a five-dollar movie for after. Something
equally amusing. But most important:
Love. Always love. The guy behind the
counter sees this as he rings us up,
embarrassed, almost afraid to touch what
we have, as if it would hurt him if he did.
Love. Always love.

Now, the regular brand. No time spent
looking around. In and out. I'm on my lunch
break. I'll get off in a couple of hours.
"Just this?" Paul at the register asks.
Yes. Just this.

SEARCHING THE PAST

Michigan
Upper Peninsula
Halloween snow
2016

We used to live a blonded life,
trying to escape the wet heat
of anxiety. A soft laugh
from both of us.
Forty-three missed calls
from each of our parents.
We cooked meals,
listened to music, we read books—
and we carried this into the night.
"We're crazy," you had said
in your black short dress,
falling in love with images.

This looks like home to me,
when the world feels empty
and I do too.

ECHOES

Drifting farther
        farther
            farther away
                until we're
back
here
where the poems began.

SINCE WE SAW EACH OTHER LAST

Another one of those dreams again.
How things could have been,
were we still happening.
Wish fulfillment.
Driving down Delaware,
you in the passenger seat,
our friends in the back,
me telling one of those
crazy work stories I'm known for.
We are on our way to a new restaurant.
We have a little dog we love.
I turn to you and say,
"We never talk anymore."
You tell me this is true.
But in this dream, we are happy,
and we are in Tulsa,
and I am still in Tulsa,
and I do hope all is well
with you.

A GLIMPSE OF THE OTHER WORLD

Pretend we never happened.
That the sky bled dry
and we had to close our eyes
to invent another universe.
That we were educated, normal,
that we were a *New York Times*
bestselling series;
"I am, I am, I am."
That we were not introverts,
that we would run with the night.
You have it. Good. Now?
We find someone we enjoy
spending time with
as much as we love
being by ourselves.

MONOLOGUE
(Adapted from *Sea Breeze Academy*)

I hate this place. I'm sorry, but I really do. I just think it's… kind of tedious? Fake? I don't know. I don't know why I keep going at it alone. But when I start to ask myself that, I also begin to ask myself why I do anything, and I'm worried that if I quit this… this *game of life*, I'll be quitting the reality I've dressed up for myself, and I'll spiral out of control. I'm currently at this point in my life where I feel like I need a change, and I don't really know what it is that I need. Like, I know I am stable in life and that I'm really not doing that bad, but I still feel like there is so much more I should be doing at this point, and then I get all flustered thinking about it. I'm attractive enough, smart, healthy and young, but I'm too much of a coward to quit. I'm worried that if I don't live my life the way everyone tells me to, that would also just be a lie to distract myself from my inherent lack of interest, with the added risk of accidentally falling for the lie.

Sometimes I'll just sleep so the time will go by faster. What kills me is not being able to do anything. Maybe I'm not ready—the end of the world. Maybe I'm selfish. Maybe things will never change back to how they were. And maybe that's perfectly natural.

We made a home here. A good one.

But this isn't the home I want anymore.

ROOMMATES

Hayley is having a panic attack in her bedroom. Kassandra and I pretend not to hear. Kassandra made some joke about Hayley being pregnant because Hayley wasn't drinking with us. Hayley didn't take it well. Hayley has this fear of being pregnant because her mom got pregnant in college; Mrs. Reynolds went into the ER with stomach pain and came out with sonogram pictures. Hayley hasn't had sex with her boyfriend in six months.

I tell Kassandra she really shouldn't have said that. It's just the two of us in their living room, on the floor, on our phones, whiskey to share. Kassandra says it's fine, she'll get over it.

I look over at Kassandra's left palm, which she tore up by digging her nails in after Jonah yelled at her yesterday and said they can't be friends. Kassandra and Jonah dated last semester. Then Kassandra turned out to be a crazy bitch. Then Kassandra assaulted Jonah in a movie theater while he was on a date with another girl. Kassandra had to resign as Student Ambassador. She no longer gives university tours. She jokes that her phone screen is brighter than her future.

I stand and go over to Hayley's door, and she's heaving and sobbing on the phone with her boyfriend. He's comforting her, and I hope she's okay. She'll pretend to be. She's president of her sorority, treasurer of Students for Sustainability, a psych and French double major, media studies minor. She has a lot going on. She can't afford the time to cry. I hate this is true.

Kassandra rises, rushes past me. I ask where—but she interrupts, something about Jonah. I try to say now is not a good time for this, but she's gone, and I think I should be leaving.

I knock on Hayley's door and whisper that I'm heading out. She doesn't seem to hear me. I see her smile at her phone. Her boyfriend, face blurred by a bad connection, smiles back at her. She's still crying. I imagine she will for a while, though I am glad, for the moment, she is okay. She is not pregnant. She is loved very much, and an engine revs, and tires squeal. I open the door out onto the balcony and watch Kassandra drive her hatchback into Jonah's front window.

Glass shattering. Someone screaming. Dogs barking distantly.

Hayley runs out to join me and asks what just happened. I point to Kassandra's car, then to Jonah, outside, his phone to his ear, shouting. Kassandra stumbles out of the car and then tries to get the phone away from Jonah. He grabs her wrists and pushes her away from him. Kassandra spits in his face.

As the campo SUVs arrive, Hayley, eyes wide, retreats back to her apartment. I follow and shut the door behind us. I ask Hayley what she thinks will happen. She says she doesn't know. I ask if Kassandra will get expelled or go to jail.

Kassandra's fine, Hayley says, laughing, rising to a hysterical pitch. She's fine! She's fine. She'll get over it.

WHITE TEE

The last frat party I went to, this one girl,
drunk on the floor and against the wall,
whined to me and our friend,
"No, it's okay if I get raped—
'cause I'm having a fun time."
And I often think about how not okay it was
for her to say that, that misjudgment,
that degree of loneliness, pain, of needing
affection or attention or sexual intimacy.
Yes, we're younger than we'll ever be.
Yes, this is the last time in our lives
we'll be surrounded by so many people
our own age—*so don't forget to live!*
But I don't think she knew
what she meant that night.
I think, each time she slipped under
the tarp that separated party from rooms,
"hedonism" from "house of,"
she was searching for something
three states away, in a home
with the porch lights on,
whispering for her to *come back safe*.
Maybe I should have said something.
Maybe that's what those online bystander
intervention courses we had to take

were all leading up to: this one night,
this one moment. To treat this seriously.
Maybe it wasn't my place to do anything—
who am I, some generic-looking white dude
with a minor in women's and gender studies,
to tell her what she can't do?
She has agency, autonomy, something.
What I know for sure is that
she later slipped in a spill of vodka
and had to be taken to the ER for stitches;
that after, she would get a Glock 17
tattooed below her ribcage;
that she was a good friend to my friend;
and I don't think she remembers this.
I'm glad nothing awful happened,
is what I'm saying.
I drank and had fun, don't get me wrong.
I guess I'm still processing, months later,
the last half hour of us being there.
A lot of running around at two a.m.,
like we never belonged in the first place.

WE ARE ARTISTS; ALWAYS CHANGING

They loved you for your long hair,
so you cut it short.
Just trying to get some life
back in you.
~~You're only helping others;~~
you're done helping others;
you only help yourself now.
But there isn't some magic URL
in your inbox—
Click Here to Discover the
Secret to Letting Go.
You are dark / pale / perfect.
Liberar, destruir,
se libre, como debes ser.
Be gentle with your new self.

LAND OF GREEN AND GOLD

We're upstairs, swaying to the music at a
Dublin pub called O'Neill's. There are
some Australian girls at the table next to
us, their hair in their faces, their hands
in the air, jeans almost off. There are some
Canadian guys taking shots at the bar,
draining their credit cards, flirting with the
girls. Everyone carries a phone, exchanging
online identities and mischievous grins.
They add a hurried, childlike excitement
to the motions. I think it is mostly truth
they are after.

I watch as you sketch the pub in your
little notebook, trying to capture the
love of the two couples dancing in front
of the singer and his two acoustic-guitar-
playing bandmates. You, with your
shoulder-length hair and gentle curves,
exposed shoulders, Swedish accent, those
fawn-like hazel eyes. Me, with my week-old
facial hair, red-rimmed eyes, those dark
and heavy bags, the tattoos you point to.
You tuck your hair behind your ear and
flash your teeth as we clink our ciders to

newfound companionship. You ask me about
my university in the U.S. I ask you about
the snow in Sweden. Together, we talk
about the metric system.

I stand from my chair, and as you join me,
you trip, and I catch you, and I hold you
tight against me. We laugh. Later, at the
hotel, I breathe out, and I ask—I ask you
if you think being busy helps combat sadness.
I just mean, back in high school and early
college, I was so moody, and now that
I have a life and things to do, I don't
have time to think about that stuff.
I tend to keep myself busy and not think
about the sadness, and so, when I'm done,
the feelings have faded. But the sadness
is postponed.

You give me a playful nod and a pleasant,
inviting smile, brightening my own face.
"People are sad no matter the country,"
you whisper. "This does not differ. But
tonight? En mycket bra kväll. A very good
evening. You keep yourself busy in a
meaningful way."

You clutch my face with both hands and
kiss me. The next morning, I breathe in,
acknowledging how happy I am here, that
there are wonderful people all over the

world and it would be foolish to hold
myself back from experiencing their
company. So I lie in that bed, in your
cuteness, your expressions, touches,
stories—and I swear, you give me
the strangest feeling of coming home.

MEMORIES, PART TWO

Years ago today, you and your friends
were bored in high school chemistry.
So you had them tape you to a chair
and time you to see how long it took
you to get free. One friend's mom left
a comment, "Is this where my tax dollars
are going?" You didn't reply.

Years ago today, you saw *Tron: Legacy*
with your friends at the movie theater.
It was winter break, and you all needed
something to do. They liked how your
flip phone—neon blue in the dark—
looked straight out of the film. You
liked how they thought you were cool.

Years ago today, you went to Costa Rica
with your mom, sister, your new stepdad,
and your new stepsister. You stayed at
a resort on the Pacific. Raccoons broke
the dishes. Iguanas roamed like the squirrels
do here. You haven't been back since, but
you tell people you go all the time.

Years ago today, you wrote a short story
you would end up incorporating into your
second novel. You were proud of the story,
as were your friends and family. Some
even commented so. Most of these people
never buy the novel. It won't sell as well
as your publisher had hoped.

Years ago today, you watched *Scott Pilgrim
vs. the World* at Rowan's house for her
15th birthday party. Ramona reminded you
of her; you had a crush on her. But Hana
had a crush on you, so you rolled with it.
After the breakup, you and Hana would never
be as close. Rowan is now happily engaged.

Years ago today, you went to Arizona with
your stepdad. You hated it. The days were
so long, and all there was were rocks and
cacti and Gatorade. Now all you want is to
go back, but you can't. It's too expensive,
you're too busy, and you never need sunscreen
'cause your laptop's not bright enough to burn.

Years ago today, you and your girlfriend
stayed with your aunt and uncle in North
Carolina as you explored UNCW. The two of
you went to the beach, to the battleship,
the gardens. You were in love. Happy.
It wouldn't last, but you both believed it.
Some nights, you miss her still.

And years ago today, before all of that,
you, your cousins, and their neighbors
were all playing Wii and making videos
to upload to YouTube. Facebook won't
remind you of this, so I will. It was a hot July.
You flooded the sandbox and played LEGOs
together. Life was great.

ROACH

I was fascinated with death
at the age of eight.
I didn't know why, just that
my dad was dangerous,
the apartment wasn't safe,
and I was so, so bored.

I used to imagine a rope
around my neck, tied to the
metal frame of my bunkbed,
the sweet sound of wind
like air conditioning...
scared the hell out of Mom.

    Here I am now,
in a cold December,
and I don't want to die.
I promise. Not today.
Dad is better, Mom is too,
and there is so much to do.

THE WIND CAN BE STILL

Walking through my high school
three years after graduation.
There's an ache in my shoulders,
this anxiety, and I'm ashamed with
my former self, so sanguine, so
vainglorious. Fake.
In college, now, I can be more
melancholy, can be contented,
can be soundless. Me.
May you too find the sureness
to be you, find that courage to
start over again.

RIVERBOAT TOADS

I fell for you not for your body
or your eyes or your laugh and such.
Not at first. It started with something
I never told anyone. Anyone but you.
Once, when I was eight, I was playing
with some bullfrogs near a creek.
Catching them, trying to make them
be buddies. I started tossing them
into the water, thinking they were
having fun, like some sort of ride.
Well, one of those bullfrogs missed the water.
Didn't make it.
I spent the day crying on and off
and had a hard time
physically letting go of that frog
and accepting that it had passed
due to me.

I told you this
during our first real conversation.
Just us. I don't why I assumed
I could trust you with this secret,
but I did, and then I waited,
and I was afraid this thing between
you and me would end right then and there

because of my previous actions, mistakes.
But to my surprise, it didn't.
We would end months later, certainly,
but that night,
you described what I had done as
innocent.
You said, "Those bullfrogs—
you just wanted them to be happy."

For thirteen years, I've been mortified.
I could not forgive myself.
You, you helped me to move on, to see past
that traumatic experience of childhood,
when everything is heightened
and the world is so daunting.
And so I say all this now because I can,
because I'm no longer afraid.
That's when I knew I had fallen for you.
That's when I knew you would one day
break my heart, and that even so,
I would grow for the better.

FELL FOR THE WRONG GIRL

You say I fell for the wrong girl.
No. Nothing wrong about her.
It would be so easy to be angry,
but I'm not. Couldn't be.
She deserves to be happy,
and that comes in many forms.
One day you'll understand.
Yes. It would take a lifetime
to begin to know her,
but this glimpse I will cherish
for the rest of mine.

LETTING GO

"Can you," Josh says from the couch, "get PTSD from a bad breakup?" then laughs at a coloring book full of penises. It's the weed. His first time. Drank a two-liter of Mountain Dew to try to suppress the coughing. No help. My only suggestion was to twist it eleven times to the right. That's how you get the perfect joint. That was the advice you gave to me.

Relaxing with this group of freshmen who thumb their phones and pretend to have similar interests. This Tuesday night, I'm the eldest. I can see my breath. A ghost who is confused about being a ghost, speaking incomprehensible onomatopoeia and exclamation marks while they, as if in a B-movie horror flick, hold responsible the wind. "Just the wind."

"Valedictorian?" Someone, at this party, referring to me. Someone I don't recognize, saying she and I went to high school together, her being two years below me. She tries to remember more. She blurts out that I wrote that one book, that I ran track, that I dated you.

But that was a long time ago. I write silly poems now. Now? All is well, I think. My life is different; I'm being purposefully vague. New subject—her major (Russian studies), why this university (scholarships), how she knows the host (roommate). She says she heard our split was messy, and it was.

I ask how you're doing.

She frowns. She says someone went to visit you in the evergreen, and that you were always out of it, and there were so many drugs, that they found you passed out on the concrete one morning, something about a literal fight club. She says I should reach out to you, maybe. Tell you as much as myself:

> "I am through with being sorry.
> I've expressed my many regrets.
> We both know how awful I feel,
> even years later. Heavy heart.
> So now, all I have left to say is,
> well, is thank you. For loving me.
> There were plenty of times
> I didn't make it easy.
> And yet you did love me.
> And yes, of course.
> I loved you."

No. You and I dated for a long time, and that was quite a time. But we made each other miserable. A lot of terrible things used to make me happy. And so I know now to leave you well alone, how apologizing would mean forcing my way back for mere performative nonsense. To recall. To relive.

She nods, asks if I want to vape with her. I pass. I think about Josh's question instead—how at last, knowing you, I know I cannot know you. How we spent that one summer lighting old fires, those night-drenched memories, waves lapping in the distance, the stars, stars and beverages, and the drinkers, young and old, fizzled and errant, sympathy we couldn't fake anymore, and that makes us unfair somehow. How we tease getting close to the water without making contact—the water that got us into trouble but wasn't even water at all. How, if you have left your life, how much of your life is left. Which life you left for. I will never know.

III. NEW HEART

BEST AVAILABLE FRIENDS

I am meeting new people today.
I want to make new friends,
but I also want to see old ones.
I approach people differently

depending on the situation;
I maintain personas.
I have this tattoo of two faces,
half of each, one eye open,
the other closed,
as a reminder to be my most
genuine self no matter who
I'm speaking with. Because

I want to make new friends.
I want to see old friends.
I am meeting new people today,
and I know who I'll introduce.

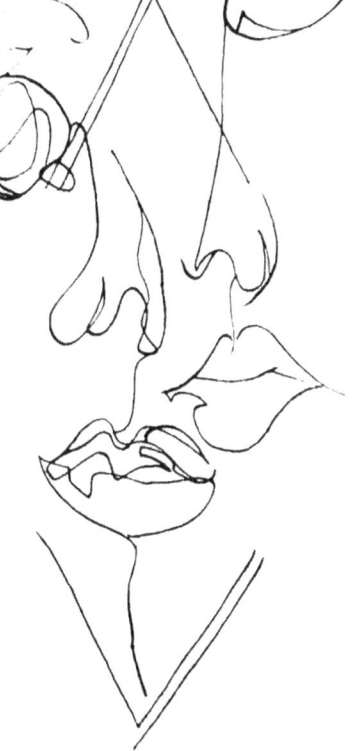

TROPICALA

Summer, summer, finally.
Beach balls and sand buckets,
sunscreen and coolers,
folding chairs, towels,
and a conga line, maybe.
Soaking up the sun, the fun.
But I will still miss you.
I won't call or text,
and it will seem like I've
forgotten,
but I haven't. Couldn't.
I do remember you—yes, you—
silent and buoyant,
in the haze of space,
as if we had all the time
in the world. I promise. So:
see you soon. If not,
see you later.

THE SILLIEST AND SOFTEST OF DREAMS

Does liking me
maybe outweigh
that fear of relationship?
That fear I kind of fear?
That fear I kind of hate?
I feel like that's what it's about.
I feel like if I touch you,
you'll run away,
and I'll crawl off
to lick my wounds.
Oh, love seems so pretentious
and stressful
and tiring.
But when I sing about you,
I flipping beam.
Because I like you.

WEIGHTED WARMTH

Baby, I'm so tired of writing about
the sad kind of love. You know. So:

When we date, I'll buy us too many
mozzarella sticks to celebrate.
I'll sing so much Disney, and you'll
join in for duets. Weekends will be
painting, poetics, random excursions.
I will couple your name with comfort,
your hair with the finest literature.
We will learn how loud you can laugh
and how softly I can whisper secrets.
There will be sand on our soles and
a spice to our tongues and shoulders.
We'll be pirates, elves, superheroes,
cops, robbers, Sid and Nancy, ghosts.

Hugs will be longer than you're used to.
Each sunlight of a weighted warmth.

TYPE

You told me once you have a type.
Does he look like me?
Oh, I hope not.

                        Baby, baby.
               Does he look like me?

DIFFERENT PERSONS

Have I been in love before?
I'm pretty sure I have,
When I was so young and behaved,
and the charts and stars were right.
Now it's  summertime,

us

Quite fine and romantic.
Have I been in love before?
Now I have to ask.
Never met someone like you.

DULCINEA

Solemnemente
sumergida
en la
tranquilidad.
Tú me prestas
los colores.
Un impacto
sería fatal.

SHADOWS TAKE ME BACK

You said,

"Take care of me, at Makeout Creek."

I'll be gentle.
And when I do
hold you under,
I won't taunt you
afterward.
We'll watch the trees
instead, shivering
in the woods.
That's where we'll be
at that shallow creek,
with this
long,
summer
feeling.

THIS FEAR OF MINE

A friend told me this one guy hits on her
by acting rude and by arguing and pestering—
like the fifth grade, she said.
I can't imagine doing that to you.
Yet here I am, tied to words, to symbols,
to heartbreak, to unsent poems…
In fifth grade, we could at least pass notes.
"Afraid of heights?" ( ) Yes (X) No
"Afraid of falling?" (X) Yes ( ) No
You know this fear of mine:
that I am this fear of yours.

TWO DISPLAYS (WHEN THE LAKE IS A MIRROR, PATIENT IS THE NIGHT)

Blue nights
in the summer
speak softly
touch gently
and watch
(so close)
these shadows
we discover
together.

———————

They held hands,
and in those hands were
photographs,
the old kind, unedited,
with years of
unmasked secrets and
imperfections; this
was love.

TOGETHER

I love you to pieces,
and it blows my mind
how special you make me feel.
I always mean it when I say
I wanna give you the world.
I want to give
a million amazing dates,
beautiful nights,
and paintings of every sky
we see together.

I could not be happier,
and I don't care when we end up
from here. And I believe in fate,
and I believe in loving someone
so uncontrollably that you feel
crazy like a kid.
I've loved you all the time,
and I'm so happy for it.

And isn't it pretty to think
we were strangers once,
and somehow,
things turned in our favor,

leaving me with this girl
I like so much.

When things seem tough,
it's nice knowing
I've still got you.
Thanks for sticking with me.
I love you madly, darling.

LOVE IS NOT AN INSTAGRAM POEM

"There is no happy poetry," you said,
complaining to your acquaintance,
"unless it's about a writer in love."

See, love is not an Instagram poem
when you're a twenty-something in college.
There are dinner dates, sure, and corn mazes.
Holding hands at the fair—yes, please.
There are more scary movie nights
and white-wine buzzes on campus than with
any of the girls back home. I'm telling you.
But love is also Jess recounting how
her sorority house might just be haunted,
and Dmitri sending photos of her cat
because she knows they'll make your day.
Love is Alex talking fanfiction with you,
Mitchell sharing novel aspirations with you,
Emma, with you, and her hopes for the future,
James and his hugs when the movie-night girl
decides on a different white-wine kind of guy.
Love is greater than the romance
we believe it must contain.
Love is the classmates who become bridesmaids,
the peers who turn into people
when we effort to know them. So I'm so sorry

you detest that there is no happy poetry
unless it's about a writer in love. Because

I am in love. I am full of love.
Happiness does show up,
and I pray you also find friends like mine.

CHRISTMAS THIS YEAR

Christmas Eve Eve at Hannah B's apartment. The tree is up, the decorations are set: LED icicles repurposed from sex lighting, stockings for the fish, a holiday wreath and centerpiece clearly on a college budget. Magentas, blues, and seasonal mirth. *Home Alone* playing on mute.

Kara singing "Sleigh Ride" on a coffee table, Tyler harmonizing, Melanie unknowingly making a magic deal with an angel in disguise, and Leahy sporting a festive toque and little else. Emily and Aedan being cute on the couch, nipping at each other's nose. Emma and Corey, graduates whom we will miss, drinking hot chocolate and reminiscing about their university days. Nick and Martin somehow wearing the same incredibly ugly sweater. Kat passing out candy canes and snickerdoodles. Elias already passed out on the ottoman.

Andy says "Sleigh Ride" is probably his favorite Christmas song. Carrie and Nathan have to think about it. Diana takes another drink. Jacob originally offers "Do You Hear What I Hear?" but Stasha says that's patronizing to deaf people, so he changes it to "Grandma Got Ran Over by a Reindeer," which doesn't fare much better. Mitchell counters with "Santa Baby." Everybody groans.

One of the Johns wants to debate whether Santa Claus is real. Hannah B calls him a coal-slinging bitch. Hannah T says, "Wasn't Santa, like, a brave and generous Turkish saint seventeen hundred years ago?" Joanna shrugs, pulls out her phone to check. Evan says that when he was in first grade, he plainly stated to the entire class that Santa Claus was dead. His parents had let him watch a documentary the night before on the real Saint Nicholas, and no one had explained that they weren't the same person. So, as one can imagine, the whole class started crying. Evan wasn't allowed to go out for recess that day, which Diane says is a questionable punishment for a six-year-old because Evan was just stating a fact.

Olivia finds the whole concept of Santa Claus disturbing. If a strange large man with a hit list, she argues, slides down your chimney at night, leaving items of mysterious origins and eating your peace offering, wouldn't that creep you out? Faith and Robert agree. Michael doesn't have a chimney. Scott says Santa Claus must be extraterrestrial then. Jourdon says aliens don't exist. Celyn says sometimes you have to be your own alien, your own spaceship. Elise wants to know what's in the eggnog. Dmitri wants whatever they're having.

This is not a poem in which I am sulking in the corner,
holding on to bitterness and a bottle of rosé. This isn't about
an ex-girlfriend, probably broken up for 'bout a month, but
sometimes a month feels like forever. This isn't about me
whining lines on how I obviously wish her only the best,
how she bubbles with warmth and radiates with excitement,
how I am glad we got to do this thing together,
how we passed a lovely summer together,

how her eyes shine brighter than New York City ever could.
In this poem, I do not look around with sullen, sunken eyes,
ask, "How many people came into our lives these past four
years?" and drunk, continue, "How many will stay?"

In this poem, all of that is behind me. A different narrative.
My mind is no longer a thunderstorm of worries.
I know now that life is full of pain
and everything comes not to stay but to pass.
High school—it came to pass.
First love—it came to pass.
Childhood—it came to pass.
And for Emma and Corey: college—it too came to pass.
That what is happening within us now is more important than
whatever has happened to us. We are good people.
And these are good people, full of love,
who will love us no matter who we are,
where we are from, or where we are going.

We are always better together.
Merry Christmas, friends.

WHITE TEE (REPRISE)

The last frat party I went to, that one girl,
now laughing and dancing with our friend,
came up to me and whispered,
"Thank you for taking care of me last year."
The hype music was too loud, but we hugged,
smiled, and then went our separate ways—
me to Tyler, Emily, Aedan, Andy, and Leahy
while Hannah B and Kara left to find boys.
I don't know where she went.
What I know for sure is that some officers
followed us to the apartment after
on the suspicion of cone-nabbing,
trying to intimidate us with fines for theft.
They left without taking names.
Emily wanted to tell them to fix the entire
university; it's all broken; thanks in advance.
So Leahy told her to fix her entire attitude;
it's all broken; thanks in advance.
Meanwhile, Tyler was all for banning those
Instagram accounts that people make
for their dogs and then write the captions
as if the dogs wrote them. And Aedan
made us garlic-breaded mushrooms
while we joked about the future—
how, in a good life, we're all vampire

mad scientists living in our abandoned
castle in the middle of the woods,
where we reanimate the dead and it is
perpetually October. Or we'll end up as artists
because that's what we do now.
I drank and had fun, is what I'm saying.
It snowed as I left, profound or perhaps not.
A lot of running around at two a.m., but still,
in that small rectangle of a campus together,
we were exactly where we were meant to be.

LONGER DAYS, SHORTER NIGHTS

Wish I'd known you three years back—
would've saved us both a lot of trouble.
'Cause I dunno, there's something about
our little road trips that've really
opened my eyes to the wonders of
the world and its many possibilities.
Is that dumb to say?
You'd tell me if it were.
God, I love your honesty.
Your sense of humor too,
like when you asked how many wheels
a car has, and I was like, four?
And you said, no, five—
don't forget the steering wheel.
Well, that I will always remember.
You'd been hurt before; same here.
Hesitant to call us anything.
"Do you get it?" you had asked,
your hand in mind, the sunset up ahead.
Yes, I said. This time I think I do.
And the road stretched on forever,
and what I could see was beautiful.

SCENE: A MEDITERRANEAN RESTAURANT BY THE RIVER, STARING OUT AT THE FLUORESCENT CITY; YOU ORDER THE FETA BRUSCHETTA AND AHI TUNA; I HAVE THE LAMB DISH AND WHATEVER YOU CAN'T FINISH; WE SHARE A BOTTLE OF WINE; WE DISCUSS DOGS, POEMS, HAUNTED MANSIONS

Yes,
  waiter,
    I'll
      have
        another
          one
            of
              those
                gorgeous
                  sunsets.

GRADUATION AFTERNOON

College, where weekends are too short for sleep
and sleep is the only thing I stay awake for.
College, where life happens so fast—
and by the time you feel settled, they ask you to leave.

Well. I won't miss the class discussions. The exams and the essays and waiting anxiously for the instructor to grade them and the worrying and attaching my sense of worth to whatever they thought. I won't miss falling asleep at five in the afternoon and then waking up at midnight to read and study and eat nothing but baby carrots and hummus for a week straight. And I won't miss the professor spending the hour lecturing over pages five and six of the book's preface that wasn't even written by the author. Words are just words.

However,
I will miss the look on Hannah's face when she successfully hosted her first college party. The scripts we wrote. Scribbled thoughts. When I was late to class because a sorority girl tried to get me to join her charity Zumbathon. Kept calling me John. I think she was drunk.

I'll miss sneaking around the water treatment plant and wondering when we'd be murdered. Taking a shot whenever the art history prof mentioned Crystal Bridges. Ranting about

No Child Left Behind and men's bathroom etiquette on more than one occasion. Ice skating. Homecoming. Snow angels. Netflix marathons and Candyland naiveté. How love manifests.

Ireland with Diane and her car, Iceland with Jess and the black lava fields, the pink skies. New Year's Eve with the high school friends and Nick's mom asking if champagne expires. Catching up with Carlos and finally having good news to report. Reading Raymond Carver for the first time, the neon of the city, those years of self-discovery.

Or when I asked her on a date and heard that enthusiastic yes. The date itself—the one with the dead spider in my hair and the horrified expression on the waiter's face. Miniature golf and dancing. Wet with sprinkler dew. Mint chocolate chip. When she kept her Converse on.

Capture the flag in front of the library with the boys at one in the morning. Dinner with the visiting author and her family before the reading. Selfies. Bonfires. Concerts. Weddings. Complimenting her so effortlessly. Romantic idealism. Watching *500 Days of Summer* from Summer's perspective—wait, no, that never happened.

Sleepy English majors. Grey Goose with pineapple juice. Sangria by the rooftop pool. The idea of soulmates, when we could fantasize about everything. Sensation, flirtation, narration: wine nights, cooking nights, cab lights, by night, by mistake. Writers bound by sentimental braids. Brown eyes. Orange sunsets. Sexy Halloween.

Goodbye to the roommate who wore the same four pairs
of boat shoes even though the state is landlocked. Goodbye
to the girl with the answers, in a floral dress and wedges. This
was January, at a house party. She and I spent half an hour
talking about Emily Dickinson and feminism before her
friends pulled her away. Never got her name.

And the country, angry as ever, beat on while we stayed put.
Bless their rampaging wild hearts. I didn't take photos. All in
the poem, imperfect but true. Yes. In this mundanity, we find
epiphany.

AZ

The year is 2039.
We're in Arizona.
There are flowers,
and sagebrush,
and some rabbits,
over that way.

Was that class we had
really twenty years ago?
How did we know?

The setting sun,
the stars between.
Dreams of loneliness,
dream.

SERENITY

You and me on a Sunday afternoon.
I walk the house in your kimono,
you in one of my plaid shirts.
We drink smoothies on the balcony,
the corgis waddling around our feet,
calling us Mom and Dad.
Inside are letters forwarded to this
address, from old friends and family,
wondering where we are.

We relax like this for hours.
We can finally see the stars.

THE EXIT IS JOYFUL

Growing up is hard.
And lonely.
But I'm learning to find happiness
in the small moments,
peaceful and loving.
A grand view of the night sky.
Full-belly laughter,
by myself and with others.
It truly is the little things.
Not how I imagined,
but good nonetheless.

EPILOGUE
(Malibu, California, half a year after publication)

I've been without words for a while now.
A lot of me was lost in you.

These days, people ask where I am
and this is what I send:
scenic drives and summer flowers.
Afternoon swims and fireside dancing
with the most wondrous new friends.
Love, I am living in a postcard—
someplace novelists can't capture in prose;
I've tried.
And some nights, just sometimes,
I read over what I once wrote. At least now
I'm not holding on to old feelings.
Just the oranges, purples, reds of the sky.
Away from expectations, but close to dreams.

Darling. Self. Here I am,
where I always hoped I'd be.

ACKNOWLEDGMENTS

These poems exist thanks to the continued support of colleagues at the University of Tulsa, in particular my fellow creative writing majors, Alpha Psi Omega, my WGS family, and the *Collegian* staff.

Special thanks to my readers and patrons, my mother and sister, my family and friends, Dr. Grant Jenkins, Dr. Jan "Prow" Wilson, Dr. Denise Dutton, Keija Parssinen, Hal Blackwell, Essence Collins, Eliza Dee, Hannah Mullen, Ethan Veenker, Brennen Gray, Cheyenne Green, Tori Gellman, Mitch Shorey, Alex Isaak, Emma Lucas, James Terrell, Jess LaPlant, Dmitri Stevens, Carlos Rubio, Maureen Haynes, Betsy Martin, Kristen Drechsler, Ataka Rhodes Royse, and Nick Miller.

Thank you to Louise Marea McKeague, Susie Inhofe, Sammy B. Karnes, LaVere Anderson, Susan Jackson Tressider, Thomas C. Thixton Jr., the Fourjay Foundation, and the Patti Johnson Wilson Foundation.

Thank you to the editors of *Stylus*.

Thank you to everyone at Peppernell.

ABOUT THE AUTHOR

Bryant Alexander Loney is the author of *To Hear the Ocean Sigh*, *Take Me to the Cat*, and the script/novel hybrid *Sea Breeze Academy*. He is a recent graduate of the University of Tulsa, and in 2018, he was the recipient of the S. E. Hinton Award in Creative Writing. You can visit him online at www.BryantLoney.com.

www.ingramcontent.com/pod-product-compliance
Lightning Source LLC
Chambersburg PA
CBHW022117040426
42450CB00006B/743